To be continued...

Becky McMullen

BookLeaf Publishing

India | USA | UK

Presentation by *BookLeaf Publishing*

Web: www.bookleafpub.com

E-mail: info@bookleafpub.com

ISBN: 9789360941178

First edition 2024

To my son.

You are the change needed in this world.

I love you more, always.

~Roberto

ACKNOWLEDGEMENT

I want to thank my sister, Jennifer, for her encouragement and support throughout the writing process from sharing silly texts and pictures to remaining silent when I needed only an ear and not a response.

I want to thank my friend Kelli F, for sharing genuine friendship, positivity and witty sense of humor.

Soliloquy

Courage embarks at mid-night,
commitment easily promised.
Conviction rules discussion,
calm soothes debate.

Composition of the day's agenda,
faithful to complete.
Charge forward with intent,
excited to succeed.

Dawn brings doubt,
draining her vivacity.
Discredit of self,
dedication disappears.

Defeat negative sentiment,
fortitude emerges.
Defy outside influence,
egress expectations.

Bold resolutions,
resilience and pluck.
Unrelenting effort,
forges triumph.

Soul Searching

Silence mastered reverberates muted.
Observant of thoughts whispered true.
Unbroken spirit, nevertheless.
Larkish in nature.
Sapience balances discernment.
Empathy demands boundaries.
Anxious sharing guarded thoughts.
Reserved, pending, trustworthy.
Courageous in execution.
Happiness is a choice.
Intrinsic realist.
Nurturing by composition.
Grateful.

On the Fence

"Sitting on the fence I see."
"Where else would you rather I be?"
"True what they say,
You've no commitment either way."
"All along, right or wrong, I'll be."

Military MoM

Cadence, revelry, muster, pause.
Unknowing, fear and worry gnaws.
Departure, prayers, yet no relief.
Prepared, engaged, the enemy falls.

Mission complete, evacuate.
No communication, silence roars.
Internal, external, fighting wars.
His strength, do not underestimate.

Homecoming, liberty, he has served.
Anxiety, frustration, often observed.
Dedication and bravery, contract extends.
Admiration and pride, emotionally unnerved.

Cadence, revelry, muster, pause.
Unknowing, fear and worry gnaws.
Son of the Military,
Freedom and justice, his cause.

Serenity

Whispers of breeze, leaves applaud –
Waiting.
Inhaled woodlands fragrance –
Appreciating.
Movement of the innocent –
Captivating.
Embrace as darkness descends –
Anticipating.
Gradients of blue, gray and green –
Painting.
Star glow spotlights souls –
Emboldening.
Stillness of observers –
Mesmerizing.
Evolution of auras –
Alluring.
Darkness diminishes –
Illuminating.
Morning light dawns –

Welcoming.
Experienced in peace –
Serenity.

Haiku

Furrowed brows, big smile
Sobs, laughter, mystery, joy
Brilliant reads include

Yuletide

Dark roast aroma fills the air.
Bold and crisp, welcoming possibilities.
Rapidly vanishing with waiting time.

Gracefully flakes feather the wind.
Swaddled carolers sprinkled about.
Evergreens laden with trinkets and treasures.

Frost nips exposed cheeks and ears.
Steaming cups, warming hands awaiting the
light.
Strong hugs, hearts filled by giving.

Spiced eggnog, mulled wine tastes of
celebration.
Dried fruit, warm nuts and sticky fingers about.
Hearty morsels, confections, invitations to share.

Silence settles the masses steady, still and all.
Hearing harness bells and children's laughter.
Bethlehem's star respires awe and light.

Sparkling eyes and cheeks outshine the spruce.
Well wishes, good cheer volleyed between.
Thankfulness and grace remain.

Tranquility

Sitting upon the river boulder,
owning utter solitude.
Chilled waters escape the falls above,
pooling in hands below.
Leaves applauding sunlight's quest,
suggestive of twilight.
Caressing breeze strokes the ground,
encouraging embers blaze.
Luminescent rainbows darting below,
unruffled tranquility.
Mellow harmonies recognized,
rhythmic and smooth.
Boundless invitations to nature,
welcome you.

At First Sight

Cute meet, first date, first kiss.
Same time, next year, still bliss.
White dress, tiered cake, celebrate.
Romantic trip, filled with love, procreate.
5 years committed, gifts of wood received, durability.
Communication, acceptance, tranquility.
10 years in, gifts of tin, resilient.
Renewal of vows, happy family, fulfillment.
Trust, patience, generosity at length.
25 years married, gifted silver, endurance and strength.
25 more, joyful harmony, good health.
50 years together, gifts golden, precious wealth.
Reminisce, first date, first kiss, delight.
We fell in love, at first sight.

Backroads

When time requires travel,
Pleasantry or not.
I always choose the backroads,
Less barriers, less fraught.

Climbing in the old 2 door,
Rust, creaks and all.
Taking a ride along the countryside,
Memories of Dad, recall.

Every ride was of importance,
This to me was shown.
The love, the joy, the laughter,
For diving backroads, sown.

Dad shared with Noah his travels,
My one and only son.
We now share rides together,
A new tradition, begun.

In the fullness of time,
Watching with my dad from above.
We will see Noah with his grandkids driving
backroads,
A tradition made of love.

Epilogue

Dad asked for a wheelchair today.
To make the journey into the hospital.
One we have walked together each week,
For the past 6 months.
So, I pushed him down the hallway.
A very hard walk for us both,
And an ending of its own.
He started talking incoherently overnight.
Confusion.
The swelling is bad.
Knees, feet, belly and left elbow.
Yet eats and drinks like a starved individual.
I cannot help him get comfortable.
Up and down, just to stand.
I am losing my mind.
Once more awake at midnight, aggravated.
He needs comfort and peace.
I need him, please Lord, to have comfort and
peace.
No food or drink in 4 days now.

Cognizant, he does as I ask and can still scream
my name.
I feel like I need to get out of my own skin.
I feel like a failure.
His only way of communicating now is to moan.
All I know for certain is, one of these hours,
I will walk into his room and not hear his
labored breathing.
And feel both heartbreak and relief.
That day was today…dad passed at 9:03 pm.

Steadfast and True

First memories of you spark summertide,
So bright, so warm, and promising.
Younger sister, teammate made,
Together in the thick of happening.

Early years spent in tandem,
Jumping rope, peddling bikes, always within
reach.
Passage of time together,
Independence, opinions and interests,
compliment each.

Nuances of early adulthood,
Separately walking different bypaths.
Yet in time of uncertainty,
Together fear our wrath.

Strong and independent women,
Different and same.
Sisters connected by birth,
Trusted friends we became.

Sincerely I thank you,
For walking by my side.
Steadfast, honest, trusting,
As support and a guide.

Equanimity

All endeavors reduce to a consistent unassuming
task.
Inconsequential, the individual striving for
success,
Or the unaccompanied, judged to have failed.
Distinctive observing, there is nought.

Reactions speak truths often words disguise,
Emotional clapbacks, sassy retorts,
Fear, anxiety, introversion, anxiety.
Awareness of emotions, often nil.

Coping creates habit, disenchantment begins,
Managing to struggling, enduring to grappling,
Subsist to battle with.

Emotion overrides intellect, understanding
defunct.

Regardless of the feeling,
The task remains,
Consistent and unassuming.
Experience moments independently, agreeable,
in harmony.

Recognize within thy self,
Emotions unique,
Be it sass or joy or sarcasm.
Internal insights acquaint emotions quelled.

Love, Roberto

I have been in awe of you since conception.
My gift to the world.
The best parts of 2 souls molded into one.
Continuously trying new things.
Not allowing my fears to deter your wonder.
Challenging me to improve myself, just by
being.
Small boy with big explorations.
Older boy with bigger adventures.
Young man with meaningful responsibilities.
A natural leader, teacher and confidant.
Voice of authority and compassion.
Forging your own way, no path needed.
Humble, reliable, respectful, extraordinary.
Aiding others with no expectation of return.
Quietly volunteering without recognition.
Simply being the best kind of human.
Standing up for others.
Leading by example.
I am so proud of you, my boy.
Love you more, always.

Calling Hours

Immersed within a darkened core,
Eyes closed, head bent,
Listening to the anguish roar,
A multitude of emotions, unspent.

The charade of fearlessness and grit,
Armor shields against faintheartedness,
With courage, bravery and daring spirit,
I present myself, nonetheless.

Agony of darkness on display,
A single light is staged,
Mourners gathered, showcase dismay,
I keep my sadness and grief caged.

The pretense of family hard to ignore,
Promises were made to remain subdued,
Irrelevant are the lies anymore,
In my heart, remembrances are true.

It's years later and yet still,
With hesitance and sorrow,
I have your ashes to spill,
Leaving my hands and heart hollow.

Reflections

I am Empathetic, you see Emotional.
I am Romantic, you see Soppy.
I am Confident, you see Cocky.
I am Receptive, you see Gullible.
I am Imaginative, you see Fantasist.
I am Kind, you see Weak.
I am Trusting, you see Naivety.
I am Introvertive, you see Shyness.
I am Loyal, you see Devotion.
I am Strong, you see Emotionless.
I am Private, you see Secretive.
I am a Realist, you see Negativity.
I am Independent, you see Stubborn.
I am Engaging, you see Flirtatious.
I am Diligent, you see Consumed.
I am Unique, you see Weird.
I am Easygoing, you see Lackadaisical.
I am Selective, you see Picky.
I am Generous, you see Extravagant.
I am Serious, you see Morose.
I am Assertive, you see Aggressive.
I see You, you see Me.

Tell Me

Why does the night veil those who admire it
most?
Why does the ocean hide its creatures?
Why does humanity sacrifice its own?
Why does time behold us?
Why does the world have only one species
where the male gives birth?
Why does the absence of good allow evil to
exist?
Why does living life for others make life have
meaning?
Why does God allow war?
Why does the heat from the sun vary in
temperature?
Why does a single moment have the potential to
alter the entirety?

Why does beauty lie in the eyes of the beholder,
but not reality?
Why does seeking knowledge make the enquirer
appear unintelligent?

Behind the Glass

The phone rings, my heart falls,
At the phone number exchange.
Worry of helplessness crowds my mind,
Nevertheless, assistance I can arrange.
No resources or a place to live,
The family has turned their backs.
Failed promises from the past,
Trustworthiness now lacks.
Thankful and gracious,
Words of praise the caller repeats.
'You saved my life,
keeping me off the streets.'
Promises of best behavior,
Words I have heard before.
The demons were quiet for 2 years,
Before winning the mental war.
Arrested, booked, and sentenced,
Only the duration has changed.
The phone rings, my heart falls,
At the phone number exchange.

Masterpiece

Vulnerable and afraid,
I invite the reader in,
To experience my emotions,
Where to begin?
Your familiarity is just that
Personal to you,
My words, my thoughts, my language,
Are known to me as true.
Each art is subjective,
Unique skills and style to share.
You like, confused, or hate it,
Of mine I do not care.
No promises of forever,
Nor happiness all days through,

Tis my bliss and serenity,
Daily I pursue.
Writing brings me peace,
Giving voice to my core,
Revealing my melodies,
Resting in silence, before.

The Farm

Fields of soybeans freckled with morning
glories,
Bugles of blue and white laced through.
Early summer sun warming the breeze,
A calf bellows for milk in the paddock.

A symphony written of children's laughter,
Cackles and clucks of chickens and geese.
Playful yips of puppies too,
Nature's melody audible to those listening.

Screen door creaks before clapping shut,
Walking barefoot to the garden.
Picking fresh cukes, tomatoes and peppers,
A finer supper there is none.

Family kickball games in the evening,
Lightening bugs in jars.
Brushing teeth, lights out,
An early start tomorrow.

Me

I sit here in the fading sunset,
Preparing for the night.
Chaos of my mind,
Never does it wane.

Appreciation for the day's work achieved,
Distressed, it was insufficient.
Sadness weighing on my heart,
Worry for those in need.

Joyful moments with my dog and cat,
Yet anxiety weighs as heavy.
Obligations yet to be completed,
Tomorrow's timetable is already full.

Startled time has so abruptly gone,
3 am appears earlier each day.
Rest should bring calmness,
Subliminal commotion prevails.

Rise from slumber,
Confident in myself.
Best efforts at achieving progress,
Today a fresh page is written.

Homebody

Overwhelming lack of motivation,
just to get out of bed.
Pressure of selecting the correct dress,
to sit solitary in an office all day.

Apprehension of addressing someone by the
incorrect name,
just to have names displayed below faces on the
Zoom meeting.

Make nice chatter in the corridor,
genuinely laughing too loud at your own story.
Escaping to the security of a closed office door,
to relax, recenter and start anew.

Deep breath, head high accompanying a
confident walk to board room,

Imposter Syndrome be damned.

Positive self-talk with a smile in place,
presentation mode engaged,
congratulations shared, success and a feeling of
relief on the exhale.

Drinks after work at the bar,

favorite seat, favorite music, favorite dinner in celebration.

Crisp walk home helps clear the head,
pup and cat excited for scraps they know are waiting.
Fleece pajamas, hot chocolate and a forgotten magazine in the lap,

settled, enjoying the melodies of night.

Library Traveler

Reverberating screams of unhappiness.
Unsensible laughter.
Raised eyebrows of distrust.
An emphatic, no!
A resounding, yes!

Discovering far away lands with adventure and
suspense.
Rafting along the river, climbing trees, enjoying
nature.
Creating worlds of magic and fantasy.
Gremlins and goblins, heroes and foes.
Learning languages and lands different from our
own.
Roman empires, Stonehenge, American Sign
Language and Mandarin.
A simple story of life on the farm or rhyming
reads as silly as Hop on Pop.
Topics of mathematics, history, aviation and
landscaping,
arts and musical instruments to choose.
Comparing bones of humans and wooly
mammoths,
while learning the differences of Archeology and
Paleontology.

Let's note the moon, stars and sky,
how the sun provides life, light and directs the
ocean's current.
Books on navigating the sea, photographing the
Fauna of Africa,
discovering Indonesia has the largest number of
active volcanoes in the world.

Romance, horror, fiction or non,
action, fable, autobiography and mystery.
Limitless opportunities exist,
for reading a book
and going places I have never been.

With Deepest Sympathies

Blackened skies with star twinkle covering her.
Tepid air unenthusiastically surrounds.
Quiet noises sound, no notice of friend or foe.
Cleansing breaths whilst clearing her mind of
thought.
Charging her soul with grounding earth.
Bended knees, head bowed, folded hands she
prays.
Asking for comfort, peace and light.
She knows the emptiness tandem to
condolences.
Helpless to carry that pain for others.
Solitude is her respite.

Walk by Faith

Eyes closed, contemplating, debating within,
whispered breath upon my ear,
'Walk by Faith.'
Eyes open wide, seeking now,
the inspirit,
to query what is known.
Yet no one to offer reason,
is found,
no part, not a bit.
Gratitude abounds,
assent to truth,
dispels suspicion.
Master uncertainty,
forge auspicious endings,
Walk by faith.